JAZZ PIANO SOLOS   VOLUME 4   SECOND EDITION

bebop jazz

Arranged by Brent Edstrom and James Sodke

T0059236

ISBN 978-0-634-02554-9

Visit Hal Leonard Online at
www.halleonard.com

World headquarters, contact:
Hal Leonard
7777 West Bluemound Road
Milwaukee, WI 53213
Email: info@halleonard.com

In Europe, contact:
Hal Leonard Europe Limited
42 Wigmore Street
Marylebone, London, W1U 2RY
Email: info@halleonardeurope.com

In Australia, contact:
Hal Leonard Australia Pty. Ltd.
4 Lentara Court
Cheltenham, Victoria, 3192 Australia
Email: info@halleonard.com.au

contents

ANTHROPOLOGY

By CHARLIE PARKER
and DIZZY GILLESPIE

AU PRIVAVE

By CHARLIE PARKER

Medium Swing

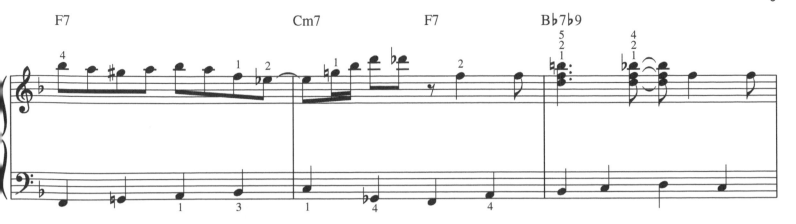

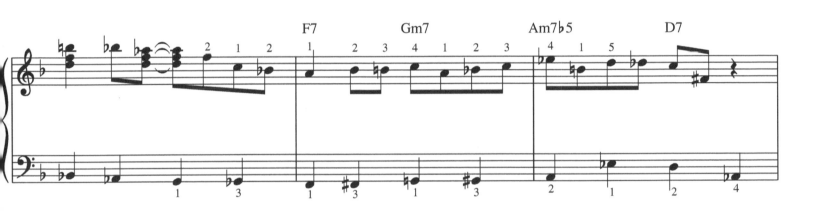

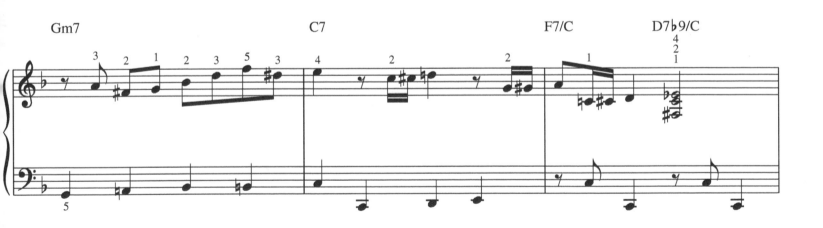

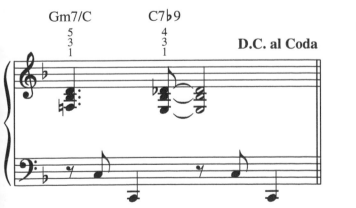

BILLIE'S BOUNCE
(Bill's Bounce)

By CHARLIE PARKER

BIRK'S WORKS

By DIZZY GILLESPIE

BYRD LIKE

By FREDDIE HUBBARD

Fast Afro-Cuban, straight 8ths

DANCE OF THE INFIDELS

By EARL "BUD" POWELL

DEXTERITY

By CHARLIE PARKER

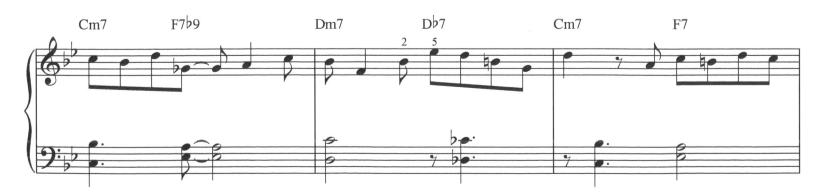

FOUR

By MILES DAVIS

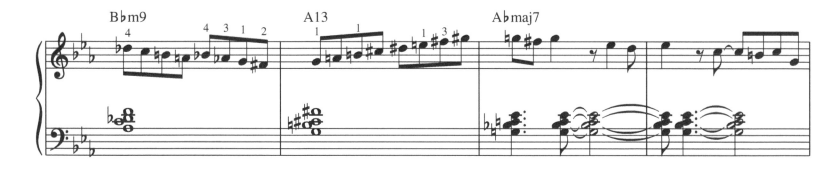

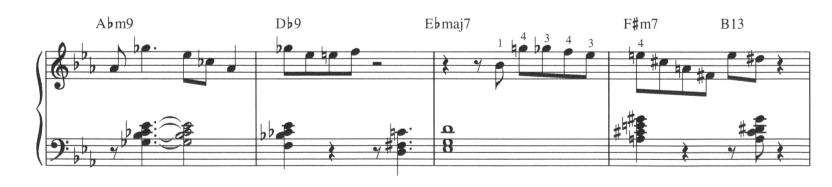

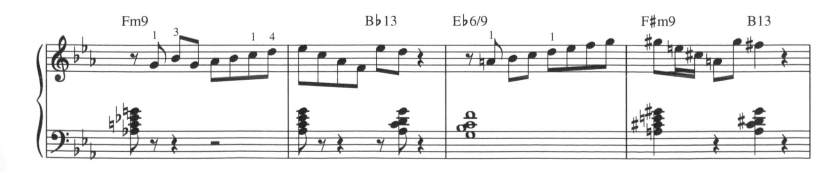

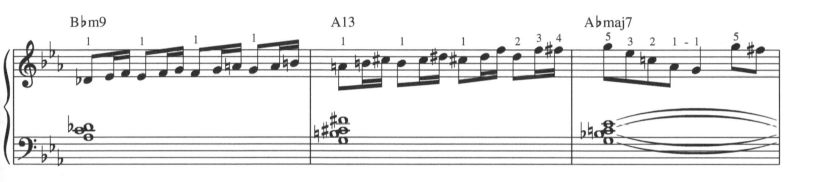

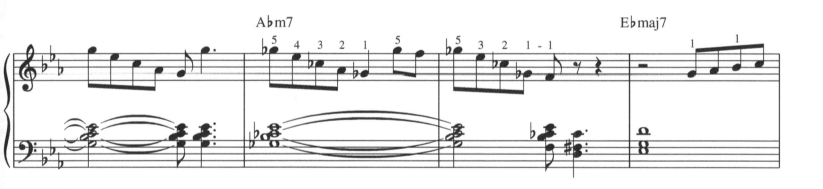

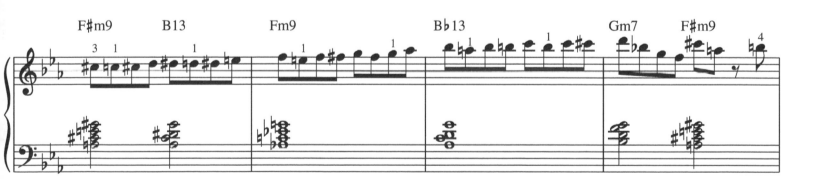

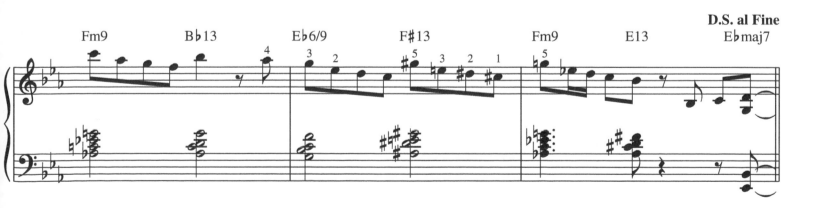

DIZZY ATMOSPHERE

By JOHN "DIZZY" GILLESPIE

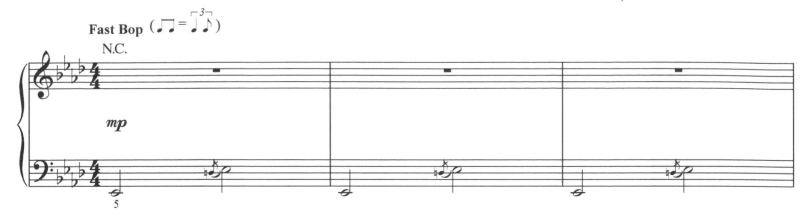

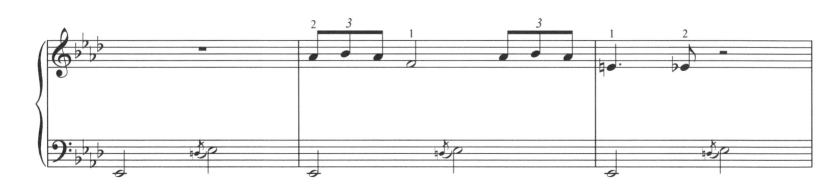

DOXY

By SONNY ROLLINS

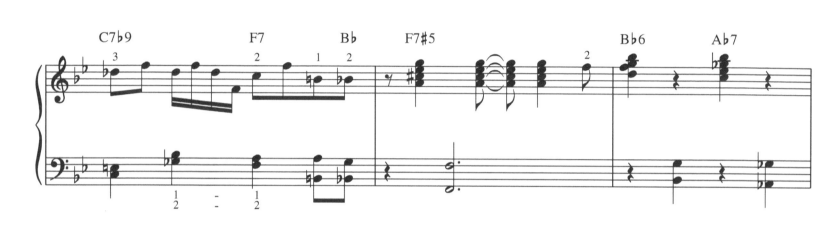

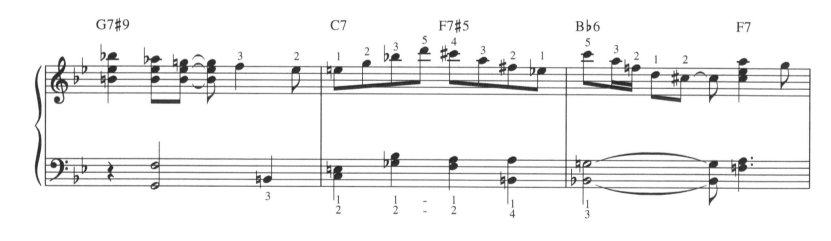

EPISTROPHY

By THELONIOUS MONK
and KENNY CLARK

GODCHILD

Composed by GEORGE WALLINGTON

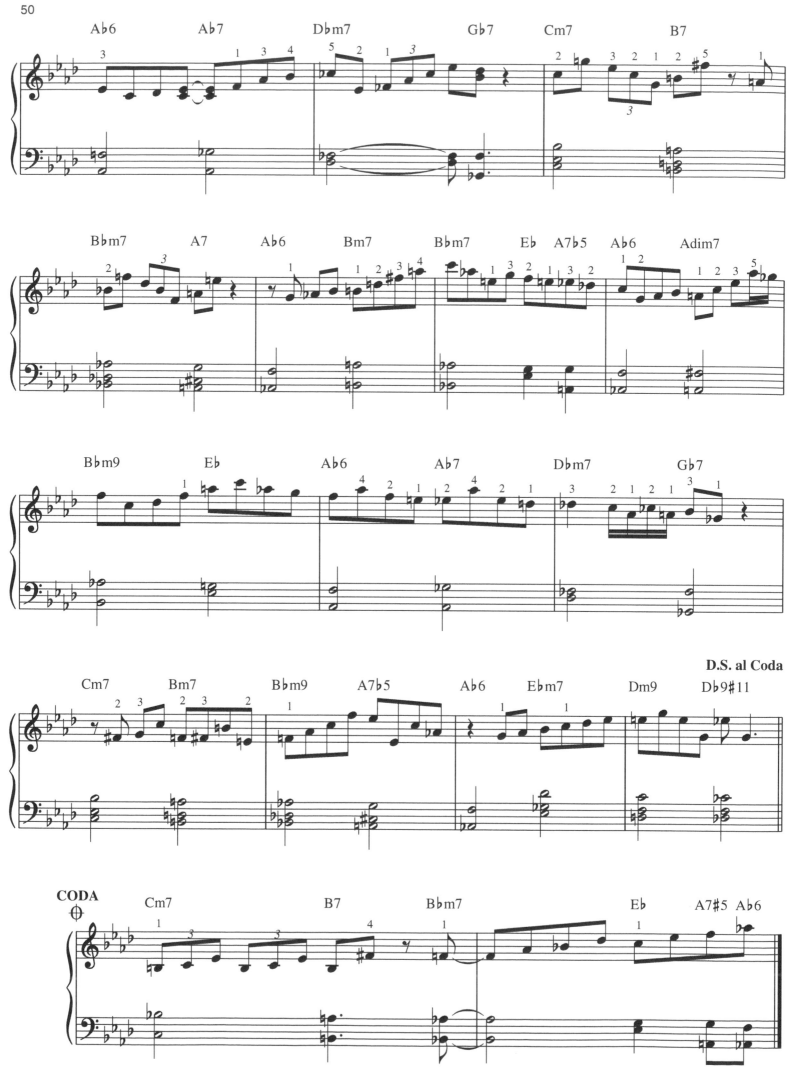

HALF NELSON

By MILES DAVIS

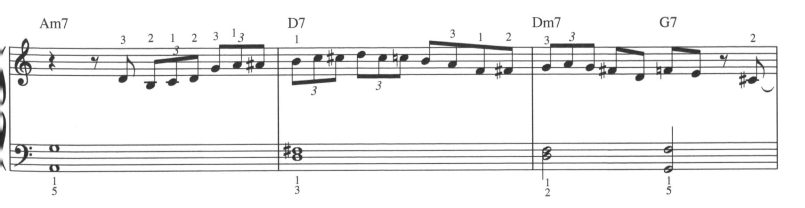

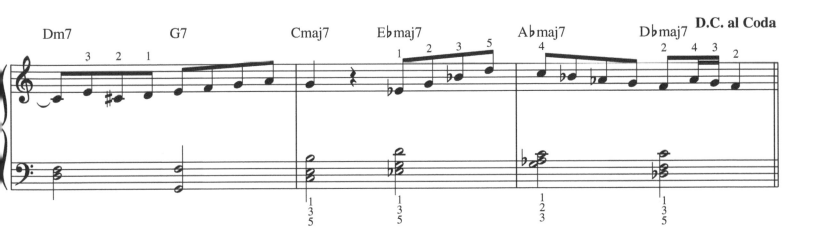

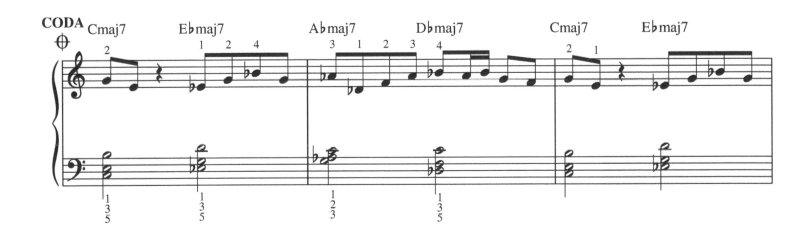

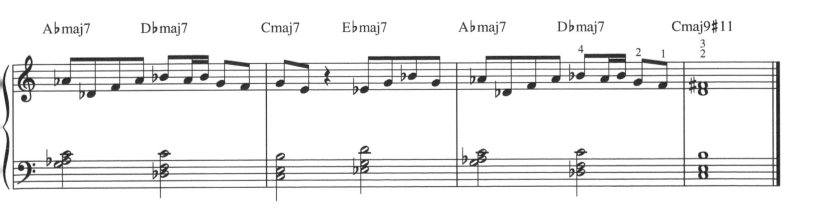

GROOVIN' HIGH

By JOHN "DIZZY" GILLESPIE

IN WALKED BUD

By THELONIOUS MONK

LEMON DROP

Composed by GEORGE WALLINGTON

LADY BIRD

By TADD DAMERON

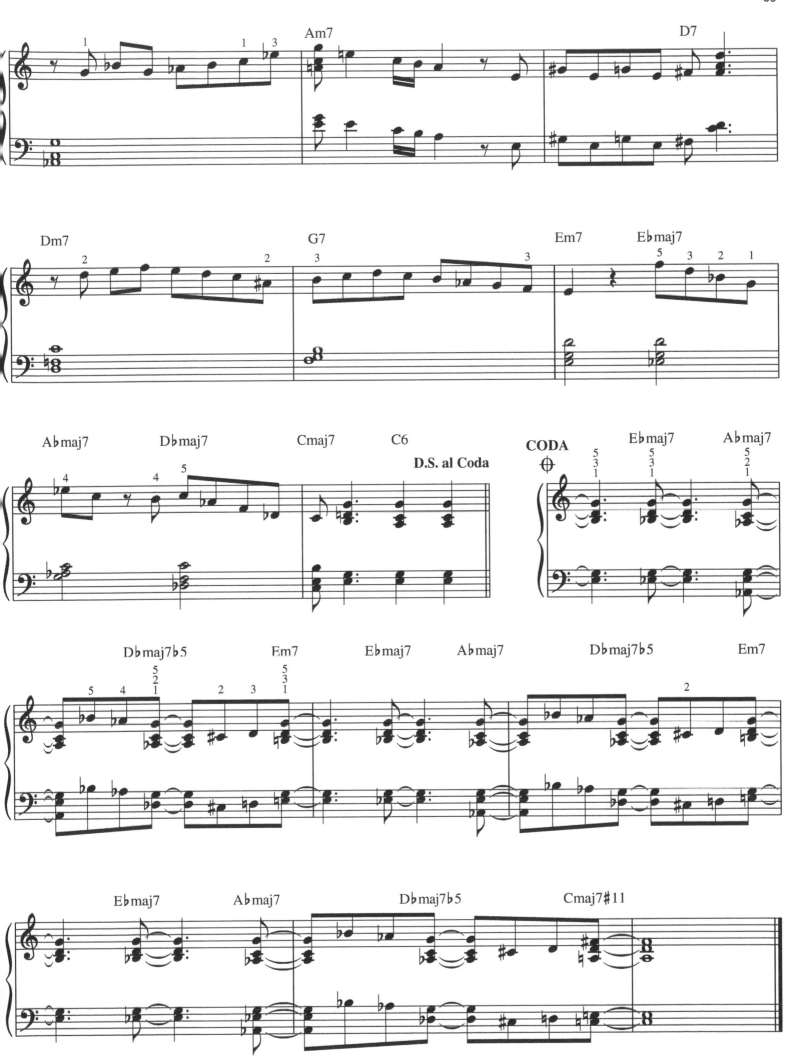

OLEO

By SONNY ROLLINS

RUBY, MY DEAR

By THELONIOUS MONK

SALT PEANUTS

Music by JOHN "DIZZY" GILLESPIE
and KENNY CLARKE

SCRAPPLE FROM THE APPLE

By CHARLIE PARKER

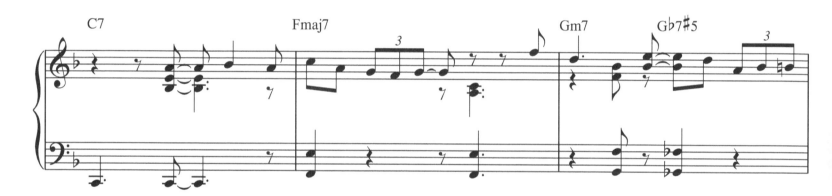

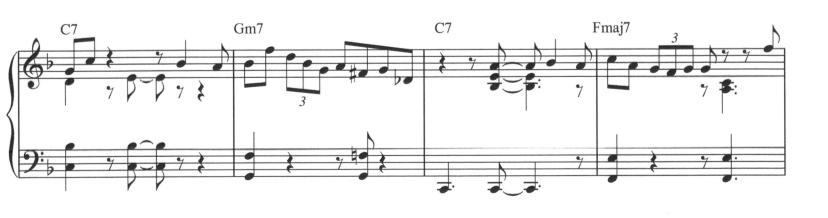

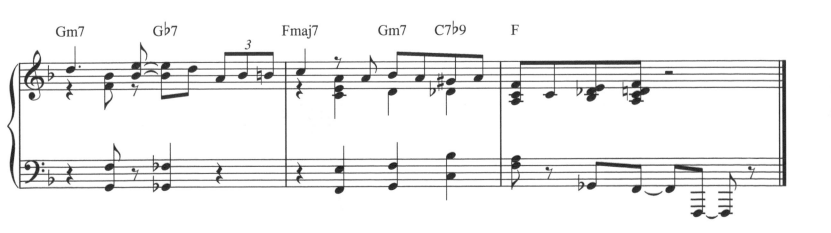

SHAWNUFF

By CHARLIE PARKER
and JOHN "DIZZY" GILLESPIE

Fast!

TEMPUS FUGIT

By EARL BUD POWELL

WOODYN' YOU

By DIZZY GILLESPIE

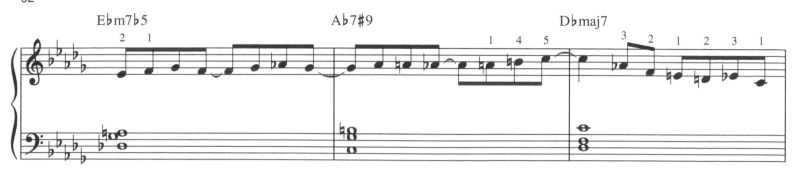

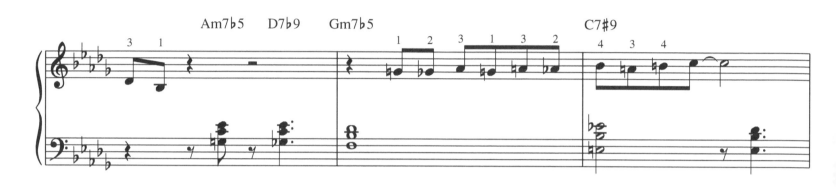

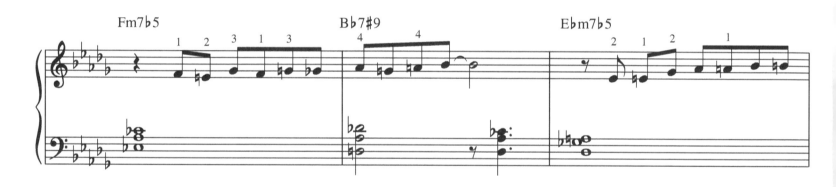

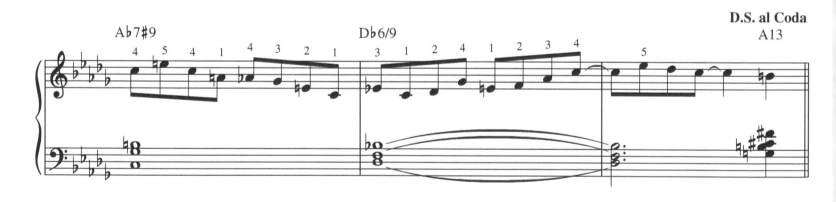

WELL YOU NEEDN'T
(It's Over Now)

Words by MIKE FERRO
Music by THELONIOUS MONK

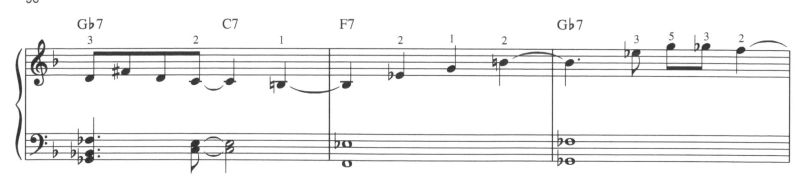

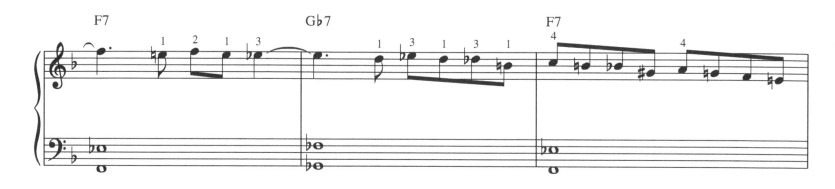

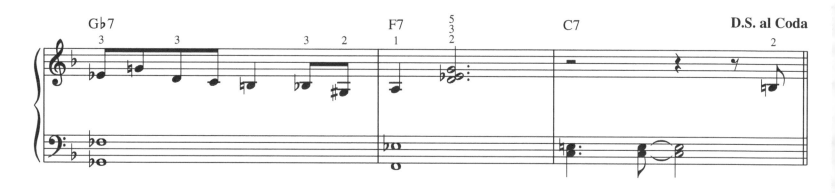